MARVEL COMICS ™

Y0-DDS-639

X-MEN ™

THE POSTCARD BOOK ™

THIRTY PULSE-POUNDING IMAGES OF THE WORLD'S MOST POPULAR HEROES

RUNNING PRESS
PHILADELPHIA · LONDON

Canadian representatives:
General Publishing Co., Ltd., 30 Lesmill Road, Don Mills, Ontario M3B 2T6.

9 8 7 6 5 4 3 2 1
Digit on the right indicates the number of this printing.

ISBN 1-56138-584-0

Cover design by Toby Schmidt
Interior design by Nancy Loggins Gonzalez
Introduction by Brian Saner-Lamken
Edited by William King

This book may be ordered by mail from the publisher. Please add $2.50 for postage and handling.

But try your bookstore first!

Running Press Book Publishers
125 South Twenty-second Street
Philadelphia, Pennsylvania 19103-4399

introduction

"The Uncanny X-Men: Children of the atom, students of Charles Xavier, *mutants*—feared and hated by the world they are sworn to protect. These are the strangest heroes of all!"

"Feared and hated by the world they are sworn to protect." That says it all. Professor Charles Xavier's band of mutant super-heroes has been battling the forces of evil for more than thirty years, and what distinguishes Xavier's group from the other colorfully clad, code-named adventurers of the comic-book world is contained in those words. Captain America? Everyone loves *him*. The Fantastic Four? They get ticker-tape parades. But the X-Men . . . the X-Men are renegades, shunned simply for who they are. No matter how many times they save the world, if you poll the man on the street in any Marvel comic he'll tell you that his family would feel a lot safer if those darned muties would just go away.

The X-Men were created by writer Stan Lee and artist Jack Kirby, mavericks who bucked the comic-book conventions of their times by introducing heroes with complex, often troubled, personal lives. Their innovative characters, including the Fantastic Four, the Hulk, and Thor, became the foundation for the fledgling "Marvel Universe." But with the appearance of *X-Men #1* in the summer of 1963, Lee and

Kirby made their strongest statement yet—a statement about the human potential for heroism in the face of persecution. Over a decade later, Marvel's mighty mutants were reinvented, supplementing the original group with new heroes for a new age. And today, the X-Men family is larger than ever before, comprising nine monthly comic-book series—*X-Men, The Uncanny X-Men, X-Factor, X-Force, Excalibur, Wolverine, Cable, X-Men Adventures*, and *Generation X*—in addition to a top-rated Saturday-morning animated series and a wildly successful toy line.

The attraction of the X-Men is simple to explain: for many of us, the X-Men *are* us. While we might not have optic power blasts or psychic powers, we do have our special, secret talents that the outside world just doesn't understand. We've all known the prejudice of our peers. And so we project ourselves onto our cool costumed counterparts, Cyclops and Phoenix and Rogue and Wolverine. *We're* mutants, and proud of it.

There's one more thing which you'll discover—or re-discover—as you flip through the pages that follow. Some of the best illustrators from the world of comics have depicted the adventures of the X-Men. As you'll see, not only do the X-Men battle ultra-powerful supervillains, but they look great doing it. 'Nuff said!

X-Men #1

The one that started it all! Published in 1963, *X-Men #1* introduced Professor X and his original X-Men, as they faced the mutant menace of Magneto!

TO:_____

_____

_____

_____

The Angel

The Angel, shown here in his original uniform, rescues a young mutant from an angry mob.

TO:_____

_____

_____

_____

The Original X-Men

Brought together under the guidance of telepath Charles Xavier, Iceman, Angel, Beast, Cyclops, and Marvel Girl became the original X-Men.

TO:_____

_____

_____

_____

Magneto

The X-Men's oldest and deadliest enemy: Magneto, the master of magnetism.

TO:_____
_____
_____
_____

THE POSTCARD BOOK™

Beast

Matched only by his remarkable intellect, the Beast's amazing agility and speed make him especially valuable in the war against evil mutants.

TO:_____

_____

_____

_____

Original X-Men versus Master Mold

The Sentinels, robots programmed to hunt down mutants, have plagued the
X-Men through the years. Here the original X-Men head into battle against
Master Mold, the center of Sentinel intelligence.

TO:_____

_____

_____

_____

THE POSTCARD BOOK

Jean Grey

One of the original X-Men, Jean Grey's telepathic and telekinetic powers make her a vital member of the X-Men's Gold Team.

TO:_____

_____

_____

_____

Magneto

Magneto's hatred of humankind has often made him a disruptive influence in the lives of the X-Men.

TO:_____

_____

_____

_____

THE POSTCARD BOOK

© MARVEL. PUBLISHED IN 1995 BY RUNNING PRESS BOOK PUBLISHERS.

Wolverine versus the Inner Circle

The innumerable minions of the Inner Circle don't stand a chance against Wolverine's superior speed and adamantium claws. Even if Wolverine is injured, his mutant healing factor enables him to recuperate faster than normal human beings.

TO:_____

_____

_____

_____

THE POSTCARD BOOK

Giant-Size X-Men #1

The appearance of *Giant-Size X-Men #1* in May of 1975 caused quite a stir among fans of the mutant band. The new team was comprised of Colossus, Cyclops, Nightcrawler, Storm, Thunderbird, and Wolverine.

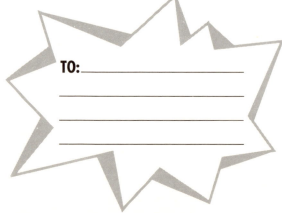

TO:_____

_____

_____

_____

MARVEL™ COMICS M

X-MEN™

THE POSTCARD BOOK™

© MARVEL. PUBLISHED IN 1995 BY RUNNING PRESS BOOK PUBLISHERS.

The X-Men

(Clockwise from top left: Rogue, Jean Grey, Iceman, Cyclops, Archangel, Storm,
Colossus, Wolverine, Beast, and Bishop)
A formidable force.

TO:_____

_____

_____

_____

Rogue

Rogue wears gloves to control her ability to steal the powers and memories of anyone she touches. A former member of the Brotherhood of Evil Mutants, Rogue has since reformed her ways and joined the X-Men.

TO:_____

_____

_____

_____

Wolverine

When readers think of the X-Men, one figure immediately comes to mind: Wolverine. Here he's using his enhanced senses of sight, hearing, and smell to track down a foe.

TO:_____

_____

_____

_____

Psylocke

Psylocke possesses a wide range of telepathic powers and deadly martial arts training. She can also focus her psionic powers into a "psychic knife" which she uses in battle.

TO:_____

_____

_____

_____

THE POSTCARD BOOK™

© MARVEL. PUBLISHED IN 1995 BY RUNNING PRESS BOOK PUBLISHERS.

X-Men

(Clockwise from top left corner: Jean Grey, Professor X, Rogue, Gambit, Storm, Cyclops, and Wolverine)
The students of Charles Xavier form an explosive, tightly-bound unit.

TO:_____

_____

_____

_____

THE POSTCARD BOOK

Storm

Storm has the power to control the weather. She has led the X-Men on a number of occasions and is currently the leader of the X-Men's Gold Team.

TO:_____

_____

_____

_____

Nightcrawler

Rescued by Professor X from a band of villagers who feared his appearance, Nightcrawler now uses his teleportation and acrobatic skills in the fight against evil mutants.

TO:_____

_____

_____

_____

THE POSTCARD BOOK™

© MARVEL. PUBLISHED IN 1995 BY RUNNING PRESS BOOK PUBLISHERS.

Wolverine

Wolverine seems to be in over his head here. While in Japan, Logan rescued a
young girl named Akiko, and has since provided for her well-being, illustrating
that even the battle-hardened Wolverine has a heart.

TO:_____

_____

_____

_____

Wolverine

Wolverine leaps into the fray.

TO:_____

_____

_____

_____

Cyclops

Leader of the X-Men's Blue Team. Though Cyclops' optic blasts can punch holes through steel, his power comes at a price; he is unable to control his optic beams without the aid of a special visor made of ruby quartz.

TO:_____

_____

_____

_____

THE POSTCARD BOOK™

© MARVEL. PUBLISHED IN 1995 BY RUNNING PRESS BOOK PUBLISHERS.

Gambit

Everything's come up aces for this X-Man, whose mutant ability enables him to charge objects with an explosive form of energy. His streetfighting prowess, though, is not to be overlooked.

TO:_____

_____

_____

_____

THE POSTCARD BOOK™

Bishop

This time-traveling 21st-century mutant first encountered (and mistakenly fought) the X-Men while in pursuit of a group of criminals who escaped from the future. When he was unable to return to his own time, he joined his heroes, the X-Men.

TO:_____

Sabretooth vs. Wolverine

Rivals for decades, Sabretooth and Wolverine have battled one another
numerous times, never resolving this most bitter of feuds.

TO:_____

_____

_____

_____

Apocalypse

Apocalypse possesses virtually unlimited might and extraordinary genius. These formidable qualities, combined with his intense hatred of humans and mutants alike, make him virtually unstoppable.

TO:_____

_____

_____

_____

Cable

Both a mutant and a cyborg, Cable's array of body armor and weapons makes him a force to be reckoned with. Though from the future, Cable now battles anti-mutant forces in the 20th century.

TO:_____

_____

_____

_____

THE POSTCARD BOOK

The X-Men

(Clockwise from top left: Gambit, Rogue, Psylocke, Wolverine, Cyclops, and Beast)

Here the X-Men's Blue Team races to oppose another foe.

TO:_____

_____

_____

_____

X-MEN™

THE POSTCARD BOOK™